31 SLAVIC BEINGS
OF MYTH & MAGIC

For my husband Scott,
without whose *wordy words*, help, and encouragement this
book most definitely wouldn't have happened.

31 Slavic Beings of Myth & Magic

A 2019 Inktober Project

Alex Kujawa
with Scott Wheeler

Wheejawa
Publishing
2022

From the Artist:

This book is a collection of drawings that I completed in the month of October 2019 as a part of the annual Inktober drawing event, during which artists from all over the world challenge themselves to post one new piece of art per day on social media. This was the sixth Inktober in which I have participated, and the third one I have turned in to a book.

I picked the theme of Slavic Beings of Myth and Magic as a means of learning more about my Slavic pagan heritage. Greek, Roman, and Norse mythologies, each had either a written language early on or a focused effort to chronicle the mythology for posterity; this is not true of Slavic mythology, which is a rich mess of confusion. Many gods and beliefs have different regional interpretations, with many overlaps, inconsistencies, and a lot of information getting lost in time. This book is not meant to be exhaustive or definitive, and perhaps no work on this subject truly can be. The beings I have illustrated are based on what I just ended up picking as my favorites, while still trying to weave a coherent story between them..

Much research and love was put in to creating this little book. Thank you for purchasing it, I hope you will enjoy it.

31 SLAVIC BEINGS
OF MYTH & MAGIC

01. Dziewa
02. Flyns
03. Dido
04. Cicha
05. Aitwar
06. Bieda
07. Trygław
08. Polewik
09. Bieliczka
10. Svarog
11. Kania
12. Rusałka
13. Wila
14. Płanetnik
15. Leśne Licho
16. Bobo

17. Chochlik
18. Leshy
19. Biełboh & Czernoboh
20. Ham
21. Meluzyna
22. Maruda
23. Perun
24. Veles
25. Graniczniki
26. Bazyliszek
27. Kwiat Paproci
28. Bies
29. Jaryło
30. Dziewanna
31. Marzanna

»DZIEWA«

DZIEWA

Dziewa is the goddess of life and longevity and the creator of all living things on Earth, including waters, forests, animals, as well as humans. Many of her various names in respective languages are derived from the word "life". Her husband is Ham, the demon Red God who created the Earth itself. Traditions hold that the blood of both Dziewa and Ham was spilled on the Earth, and Dziewa pulled humans from the ground, and, with the help of a spark of life from the heavens, fashioned men in to the image of Jesse (the one original Slavic God, often understood as a version of Jupiter), and women in to her own image. She was worshipped in parts of Central and Eastern Europe before the spread of Christianity in to the area. She is usually depicted as a naked maiden holding an apple and a wreath, with leaves in her hair.

OTHER NAMES:

Zibog, Zhibog, Siebog, Zhiva, Ziwa, Żywia, Zywi, Živena, Żiwia, Siva, Siwa, Sieba or Razivia

FLYNS

FLYNS

The Slavic God of Death, who answers to the God of the Underworld, Peklenc. He brings the souls of the dead to the underworld, similar to Charon of Greek mythology. Perhaps uniquely among Gods of death, Flyns was also known to bring people back from the Underworld to rejoin the realm of the living, though temporarily. This was not seen as a good thing, and has some similarities to the Eastern concept of reincarnation. Souls would be brought back to life in order to be denied access to paradise, and forced to endure life again and again until that soul is deemed worthy to be granted access to Heaven. Flyns would also sometimes bring the dead back to the living world briefly in order to visit their loved ones. He is depicted either as an old man or a skeleton, a staff or lit torch in one hand, a lion resting upon his shoulder, standing with one foot on a large stone or flint.

OTHER NAMES:
Flins, Flyntz

DIDO

DIDO

Dido is an obscure Slavic type of guardian spirit that typically resides in lilac trees. Dido is a small, awkward looking creature, about one foot tall, with a small mis-shapen body, long hair and beard, and a disproportionately large head with a stupid smirk on its wrinkled face. If you ever see a dido he will remain very still like a statue. It will take care of the grounds of a farm or estate, but will never enter the buildings. Its main function is uncertain, but it likely guards its area from other spirits or demons who would want to harm the grounds or the living beings residing there, including humans, animals, and crops.

OTHER NAMES:
Diduch, Dyduch

Cicha

CICHA

Her name means "the silent one" and she is the personification of child mortality. She is a demon with the appearance of a little girl wearing a white dress, her skin pale, her protuberant eyes cold and dead. She wears a wreath of red poppies and a blood red ribbon or handkerchief in her black braided hair, and she holds a black steel rod in her hand. She comes out from fir forests, through the fields, flowers wilting and grass burning underneath her feet. She likes to visit cemeteries where she can dig up bones from old graves. She will seek out playing children, whom she will get close to until she can touch them with her rod. Whomever she touches will convulse and fall dead, their cheeks turning black like coal.

The origins of Cicha are unclear.

»AITWAR«

AITWAR

A Slavic creature that resembles a winged snake with a bird-like head, and is sometimes compared to a small guardian dragon. An Aitwar will fly in to people's houses at night through their chimneys in order to steal food and other objects; they are especially fond of potatoes, but will also steal hay, clover, grains, money, and even small appliances or other objects from around the kitchen. When escaping while carrying stolen goods, the Aitwar is said to glow or to emit sparks, causing it to take on the appearance of a shooting star, for which it would often be mistaken. It is possible to keep an Aitwar as a pet by leaving an offering of food in a warm spot in one's house, which will cause it to bring its stolen objects back to you.

OTHER NAMES:

Ajtwar

BIEDA

BIEDA

An immortal demon that plagues humanity with emotional suffering and worry. She takes the form of a very tall and extremely skinny and bony woman, with abnormally pale skin and deep red lips. She wears dirty clothes made of spider-webs, and a wreath of old, dry ferns. She dwells in fields of trees, and will sometimes inhabit a household cooking pot, during which time she will occasionally make a sad squeaking sound when the pot contains food, or if something is being cooked in it. Her name comes from the words for "poverty" or "unhappiness".

OTHER NAMES:
Bida

TRYGŁAW

TRYGŁAW

An ancient Slavic God of trinity, sometimes on its own in a self-contained trinity, or sometimes included in the ancient Slavic pagan trinity that also contains Jessy (the God of light) and Halu (the word of creation). Trygław is said to be both male and female at the same time without being either, and has three heads, one male, one female, and one of uncertain or indistinct gender. Trygław created other Gods by ripping off its own heads, each head would spill a different color of blood, and each separate color would create different kingdoms of Gods. From its spilled red blood was created the kingdom of Earth, from its spilled black blood was created the kingdom of the Underworld, and from its spilled white blood was created the kingdom of Heaven.

Other Names:
Trzygłów, Trigla, Tryglav

Polewik

☙ POLEWIK ❧

Of Russian origin, Polewik is a demon of the fields, especially wheat fields, for which they care and in which they live. They are about a foot tall with dark earth-like skin, and wearing a simple white tunic, pants, and boots made of hay. They have long hair and beards not of usual hair but of wheat, grass, and hay. They will hunt and scare birds away from their fields, and are most active around noon and just after the sun sets in the evenings. Human-Polewik interactions are usually unpleasant for the involved humans. The Polewik will stomp all over a human who falls asleep in their field, suffocating the unfortunate person; they will try to confuse a conscious human in to getting lost in the field; and drunken humans will usually end up being killed by the Polewik. Since they are beneficial to the field, farmers usually try to keep the Polewik around by leaving a few eggs or a mute rooster within their field. During harvest time, the Polewik needs to run and hide away from the harvesters. Farmers will usually keep the last bundle of harvested wheat for the Polewik, singing while bringing it to the farm and placing it somewhere safe so the Polewik will have a place to stay until Spring.

OTHER NAMES:
Polewoj

Bielioz Ka

BIELICZKA

Bieliczka, the white lady, is the resident demon of the Wieliczka salt mine near Kraków, Poland. The Wieliczka salt mine is one of the oldest and longest-operating salt mines on the planet, with a centuries-long history starting in the 1200's and remaining operational until 2007. Bieliczka is a being that is often heard and seldom seen. She is usually described as a beautiful woman dressed in fluffy winter clothing, with dark hair and pale skin. She has been heard to sigh and weep within the mine. It is said that the various water leaks that appear around the walls of the mine are caused by her tears. Stories tell that she was originally a young woman who fell in love with a worker at the salt mine. She would spend time with him in the mine, walking along its corridors. He was called away to fight in a war, and promised that they would be together forever when he came back. She waited for several years, and decorated the walls of the salt mine in preparation for his return, which never came. She apparently became unable to leave the mine of her own will. There is a story of her spirit appearing to a man and asking him to carry her from the mine, he attempted to, only to find that she became heavier with every step as they approached the exit, until she turned in to a pile of pure white salt in his hands.

Other Names:
Płaczka, Bielinka, Ojdola, Biała Pani

SVAROG

SVAROG

A Slavic deity of enigmatic origin, his name can be found in only a single historical source, the "Hypatian Codex", which is an Old Slavonic translation of a Byzantine account of Egyptian history, wherein the translator used "Svarog" in place of "Hephaestus", apparently in an attempt to use names which would be familiar to his target Old Slavonic audience. From what information is known, Svarog is the God of fire and of the forge, and is said to have given metal weapons and tools to humans, who were only using wooden and stone tools prior to this benefaction. He is the father of Dazbog, the God of the Sun, whom Svarog seems to have fashioned rather than sired. Svarog is also sometimes associated with Svetovid and Perun, but the nature of these associations is unclear. Despite his uncertain origins, Svarog has a lasting legacy on Slavic culture, lending his name to several cities in different countries, and also to a variety of words involving fire in several Slavic languages. He is worshipped as the creator deity by certain modern-day pagans.

OTHER NAMES:
Swaróg, Jarog, Rarog, Tvarog

Kavia

KANIA

A child-abducting demon that takes the form of an abnormally gorgeous young woman, with milky white skin and usually with long black hair. She is associated with clouds and mist, travelling within them and surrounded by them. In the evenings or at night, she will descend to kidnap lonely or unsupervised children. She uses her charming nature to enchant the children in to trusting her and going along with her as though she was their mother. Once a child embraces her, she will grab on to them and surround them with her clouds and mist, after which she will fly away with the child and take them far away, deep in to the wilderness, from which the child will never return.

OTHER NAMES:
Kaniora

Rusalka

RUSAŁKA

Rusałka is a water spirit in Slavic folklore. Sometimes translated as "Mermaid" though they are in fact entirely different entities. Historically held to be benevolent spirits who brought moisture to the land during the growing season, the last few centuries have seen the rise of more sinister stories. A Rusałka will appear as an extremely beautiful woman, and she will lure men to the water where she then drowns them, sometimes while tickling the man and laughing. Some traditions state that the Rusałka cannot entirely leave the water, and must at least keep her feet submerged, while other tales have them fully capable of mobility beyond the water. Their activity is often viewed as seasonal, being more active during different times of the year, with regional variation.

OTHER NAMES:
Rusalka

Wila

WIŁA

Wiła or Vila are a type of fairy or nymph that are found in the folklore of the South Slavic countries and in Slovakia. They are the souls of lost women who died unbaptized, or betrothed ones whose lives tragically ended before marriage. There are different varieties said to inhabit the different areas of water forest and air, and the air Wiła can additionally take the form of mist. They appear as extremely beautiful nude or translucent-clothed women, often with wings, but are also able to turn themselves into various animals such as horses, swans, falcons, and especially wolves. They usually live in groups and enjoy dancing in the moonlight. They have magical levels of charm, and easily seduce men. They are famously capricious and quick to rage, which makes them very dangerous to men that meet them. There have been tales of Vilas using their magical charms to make men dance to death for their amusement.

Other Names:
Vila, Wila, Samowiła, Samodiwa

PŁANETNIK

PŁANETNIK

Płanetnik are sky demons and giants that cause the clouds to move in the skies. It is said that the clouds are all connected by ropes, and the Płanetnik pull on the ropes to drag the clouds around. As such, they are mostly responsible for the weather, and it is of great importance to farmers to appease the Płanetnik. They are described as giant, muscular, very hairy men with old and tired faces, though when interacting with humans directly they will appear as a tall man wearing a large hat. Farmers will throw flour to the wind or burn flour in a fire in order to offer it to the Płanetnik. A successfully befriended Płanetnik will not only grant you good weather, but will also warn you of approaching storms or forthcoming droughts. They originate from the souls of men who have died suddenly, usually those who drowned or committed suicide. Large storms in the skies have been attributed to the Płanetnik having battles with dragons. They are also known to take serious interest in their leisure time, enjoying the smoking or chewing of tobacco, and drinking hard liquors.

Other Names:
Chmurnik, Obłocznik, Poświst

LICHO

LEŚNE LICHO

Licho is a demon which is either the same name for two separate entities, or an entity which can take two separate forms. One is the form of a cyclopean old woman, the other is a small squirrel-like "goblin" creature with large round eyes, which is known for causing mischief. This latter form of the Licho, the "Leśne Licho" is small, shaggy, and troublesome, though less dangerous than the one-eyed old hag variant. They inhabit fields and forests, and are known for various mischievous deeds such as breaking dinner plates, loosening axe blades, adding ash to flour, or hiding small objects around the house. There are tales of Licho jumping on to the backs of victims and grasping on to their necks, refusing to let go. In desperation, the victim will wade in to water, hoping to drown the Licho, but ends up drowning themselves instead.

OTHER NAMES:
Licho, Likho, Liho, Gremlin

BOBO:

Bobo is a small creature resembling a small, ugly owl, stories of which were used to frighten children in to behaving at night. The Bobo would perch on the end of a child's bed and attempt to suck its blood, no matter whether the child was good or bad, and its activities were aimed particularly at tormenting children. The name originates from the Latin word "bubo" which is their name for the Eurasian Eagle-Owl. Said to be nocturnal like the owl, it favored dark places during the day, such as basements or rarely-visited attics. To get rid of a Bobo, one should leave out enough food for it to satiate itself, so it does not need to suck on a child's blood for nourishment.

OTHER NAMES:
Bobak, Bebok, Bobok, Babuk, Buba

Chochlik

CHOCHLIK

A house spirit that looks very much like an ordinary housecat, but can also become invisible. A Chochlik usually has a longer tail and limbs than a regular cat, highly expressive eyes with prominent double eyelids, greater strength, and unexpected outbursts of energy. They are mischievous and like to play tricks on people, and will also eat some of your food and supplies. If you treat a Chochlik well and keep it fed, then it will defend your house from other potentially harmful spirits. If you mistreat a Chochlik, then it will go on a rampage around your house, knocking things off shelves, breaking dishes, and even overturning furniture. Given that they look so much like common domesticated cats, it is best to treat all cats well, lest you accidentally anger a Chochlik.

→→LESHY←←

LESHY

Leshy is a guardian spirit of the forests. They are usually humanoid in shape, often being portrayed as a very tall man with horns, bright green eyes, and a beard of vines or other plantlife. They are often accompanied by bears and wolves, and they can take the form of these or any other animals or plants that reside in their forest, though their bright green eyes remain as a distinguishing characteristic during transformations. Their height is also variable, in the middle of the forest they are as tall as the trees around them, but they get progressively smaller as they near the edges of their forest. Leshy were known to be unfriendly toward lumberjacks and hunters, who must take caution when engaging in their activities in a Leshy-protected forest. They can be tricksters who cause humans to get lost in their forest, they do this by imitating the person's own voice, though eventually they will get bored and allow the human to leave. A forest will typically have one male Leshy and his family. Two male Leshy in the same forest will fight each other for dominance, and folklore tells that broken trees in the forest are the result of such battles.

OTHER NAMES:

Leszy, Leshi, Leszy, Leśnik, Leśniczy, Lasowik, Boruta, Borowy

BIEŁBOH

CZERNOBOH

BIEŁBOH & CZERNOBOH

Biełboh the white God and Czernoboh the black God are interesting figures in Slavic mythology. More recent absolutist influence from Christianity has reduced them to being simply good and evil adversaries, but their original nature is more nuanced than this. Biełboh and Czernoboh do indeed represent opposites, light and dark, good and evil, but their interactions are viewed as balanced, complimentary, and necessary, similar to the Chinese Yin and Yang. Chernoboh stimulates Białboh to action, and Białboh keeps Chernoboh in check. It is said that they were born from the white and black blood of Trygław, respectively, and each command a pantheon of seven other deities. Above them was Ham, a Slavic creator God who settled disputes between them, further solidifying their balanced nature. Both Biełboh and Czernoboh have lent their names to numerous places in the Slavic lands.

OTHER NAMES:

Bielbog, Belibog, Bielobog, Bjjelbog, Byelobog
Chernobog, Chernibog, Crnorbog, Czernibog

HAM

HAM

Ham is a supreme deity who created the Earth as well as "a unity of all opposites". He is called the Red God, and often referred to as a demon god and "Lord of Infernal Hosts", likely owing to Christian influence on history. Ham is said to have ram's horns on his head, which represent forgiveness, patience, and strength. The horns curve downwards, symbolizing his interest in, and care for, the Earth. The two horns also represented his power over Biełboh and Czernoboh, and the balance between the two. According to at least one source, the city of Hamburg, Germany was originally named after ham as "Hamboh" and was changed to "Hamburg" after the rise of Christianity in the area. Ham was often likened to Jupiter by later historians, with the name of "Jupiter Hammon" being given in some studies of old Slavic faith.

OTHER NAMES:
Hamboh, Hambog, Bohem, Erjawoboh

MELUZYNA

MELUZYNA

A winged half-woman, half-fish creature said to have traveled to Silesia from the warmer climates to the South, and never grew accustomed to the colder temperatures. She can be found begging while crying and wailing miserably, asking for food for her and her offspring, especially in the winter. She will tend to find the warmest spot she can, such as beside a chimney. People may leave her bread or flour, but it is a bad idea to invite her inside your house, as she may end up tearing apart your kitchen in a fit. Before fleeing to the North, she was apparently married to a prince, who, as part of their marriage agreement, was to allow her solitude in the bathroom for one entire night each week. They had a happy life and were very much in love, but the prince's mother became suspicious of Meluzyna and convinced him to spy on her one night, suspecting evil-doing of some sort. He did so, and spied his wife in the bath in her half-fish form. She shrieked, horrified at his betrayal, and fled Northward on her wings where she continues to live her sad, cursed life.

OTHER NAMES:
Melusine, Melusina

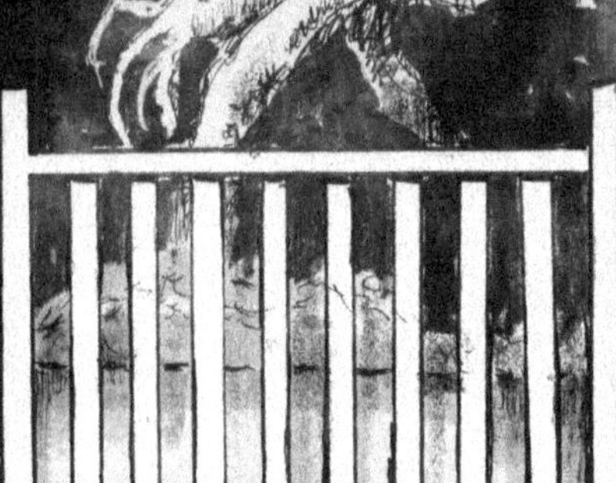
MARUDA

MARUDA

Maruda is a demon who specializes in the tormenting of young children, particularly infants still in the cradle. It can take the form of an old hag of a woman, but can also be simply a disembodied voice and a formless pinching being inflicted on the baby. The Maruda will terrorize the baby to the point that nothing will appease it, not its favorite toys or being coddled by a parent, causing many a sleepless night for the afflicted family. There were several methods a family could employ to attempt to end the Maruda's torture; placing a bowl of water containing spoons, spindles, and a ball of thread, next to the baby's cradle was said to cause the Maruda to become distracted and begin playing with these objects instead of irritating the baby. Also, placing nine rag dolls inside the crib could potentially cause the Maruda to become confused, not certain which "baby" it should be frightening. Usually though, nothing would work permanently, and the parents must wait until the Maruda goes away and their baby stops crying on its own, an experience shared by parents of young children to this day.

PERUN

PERUN

Perun is usually considered the head God of his pantheon, and is the God of the sky and of lightning, to which he grants his name (compare Polish "piorun" for "lightning" which takes its name from Perun). Perun is generally viewed in opposition to the Slavic deity Veles, God of death, water, the afterlife, and the underworld. Objects struck by lightning were considered to be blessed by Perun, the result of his attempts to smite Veles, and were treated as tokens of power and good fortune. He is associated with a sacred oak tree, and represented by an eagle perched atop the tree's highest branches, watching over the world. In South Slavic tradition, there is a ritual of casting out vipers, to which Perun is viewed as being opposed, in order to bring forth the rain. Compare to Thor of Norse mythology, though Perun's weapon and symbol is an axe instead of a hammer.

Other Names:

Parun, Peron, Porun, Piorun, Peraun, Parom, Perusan, Prone, Prohn, Pyron, Perone, Peryn, Perin, Prono, Percunust

VELES

Second in power only to Perun, and viewed as opposed to him, Veles is the God of death, water, the afterlife, and Navia (the land of the underworld), among other things. Not universally viewed as evil, Veles is also the God of cattle, and will protect the herd from wild animals. Veles is variously also known as a God of prosperity, of foretelling, and of arts and crafts. Later Christian influence imposed the dualistic and absolutist nature of good and evil upon Veles and led to him being viewed as an evil God by some. In actual tradition, he is much more ambiguous, as is common in Slavic mythology. He is mischievous and makes trouble, variously said to have stolen Perun's wife, child, or cattle. The battles between Perun and Veles were the catalyst to bring about the change of seasons in old Slavic mythology. As Perun is symbolized by an eagle atop the sacred tree, Veles is the serpent at its roots.

Weles, Voros

GRANICZNIKI

Sometimes in the evenings, just beyond the edge of the village, people may see mysterious shimmering lights moving quickly along the border between the village and the fields. These are the Graniczniki, mysterious deformed figures moving around very quickly but aimlessly, never coming too close to the villagers. Some will look like a human with a glowing head, others may have no heads at all, and yet others may take the form of deformed children that appear to be holding a glowing light of some kind. What they all have in common is the mysterious light by which they are seen in the night. They seem to take no notice of the living world, and do not react to human presence. It is said that they are the spirits of villagers long dead, or perhaps just the imprint of a memory of these people. One place these Graniczniki have been seen is around the village of Nowy Targ, in Southern Poland near the Tatra mountains and the Slovakian border. Their name comes from "granica", the Polish word for "border".

OTHER NAMES:
Granicznik, Graniecnik, Graniecniki

Bazyliszek

BAZYLISZEK

Called the king of serpents, the Bazyliszek is said to be born of an egg laid by a seven-year-old rooster, incubated a further nine years by a toad or a snake. It dwells in dark tunnels and feeds on mammals of all sorts, and is deadly of venom, breath, and especially gaze, which has the power to turn its victims in to stone. Specifically in Slavic mythology, there is the tale of the Bazyliszek of Warsaw that lived in the underground beneath a certain house in Stare Miasto (Old Town). There are several versions of the story, but generally, the Bazyliszek killed the daughter of a local blacksmith, who asked a man to dispatch the Bazyliszek in kind. This person descended to the basement with a mirror or a suit covered in mirrors, and apprehended the Bazyliszek by using its own gaze against it, to the relief of the blacksmith and the citizens of Warsaw. Today, a restaurant called Bazyliszek occupies the very same legendary house where this encounter supposedly took place.

Other Names:
Basilisk, Basiliskos, Regulus

Kwiat
Paproci

⇶KWIAT PAPROCI⇷

The Fern Flower (Polish: Kwiat Paproci) is a legend and tradition found in Slavic, Baltic, and Nordic cultures. Ferns are not flowering plants, but according to legend a fern flower will bloom once on the night of the Summer Solstice (Noc Kupały / Noc Świętojańska), the shortest night of the year. Young couples will go in to the forest together on this night to look for the Fern Flower, the young woman will wear a wreath on her head, and if they leave the forest with the young man wearing the young woman's wreath, then they have become engaged to be married. There is a legend of a peasant man who found the Fern Flower, which spoke to him, offering worldly riches on the condition that he would be unable to share his wealth with anyone else. He agreed, and the Fern Flower took root in his heart. He lived a lavish lifestyle while his family and loved ones remained in poverty, eventually starving to death. This broke the man's heart, and he died. Swallowed up by the earth, the Fern Flower is said to bloom on the spot where he perished.

Other Names:

Fern Flower, Papardes Zieds, Sõnajalaõis

Bies

Bies (plural Biesy) are Slavic demons that embody all nebulous evil in nature. They can influence humans or even take possession of human bodies for their evil purposes, which usually drives the victim insane. Animals can warn of the presence of a Bies, such as the untimely call of a rooster, or a cat hissing, and travelers are advised to turn back at these omens. A Bies will often haunt rural crossroads, where they are said to be guarding buried treasures nearby, but they usually live in bogs, deep lakes, and ancient forests. The word "bies" is present in many Slavic languages, usually in conjunction with rage, madness, or evil influence. Christianity later branded Biesy as the devil, or merely as the wiles of Christian-style demons.

OTHER NAMES:
Bis, Běs

JARYLO

Jaryło is a Slavic God of Spring, springtime sunshine, fertility, plantlife, and war, specifically victory in war and the resulting peace that comes after victory. He is also tied in to a life-death-rebirth cycle along with Dziewanna and Marzanna. Commonly depicted as handsome, youthful, athletic, and blond, mounted atop a white horse, holding a bundle of wheat in one hand and a severed head in the other. Usually counted as a son of Perun, he was stolen and raised by Veles in the underworld, where he tended his adoptive father's cattle. His return from the underworld in the springtime is associated with the return of life to the fields, and his death or return to the underworld in autumn is associated with the "death" of the crops at the harvest.

Other Names:

Jarilo, Jarylo, Yarylo, Iarilo, Gerovit, Harewit, Herowit, Harwit, Jurowit, Jarowit

DZIEWANNA

DZIEWANNA

Dziewanna is a Goddess of the hunt, forests, and the wild aspect of nature. She is often depicted on a black horse, riding or running with deer or wolves. To the forests she favors she will bring richness of life and healthy clean air. She is also the twin sister of Jaryło, as well as his lover. The tale goes that upon Jaryło's return from the underworld in the Spring, he meets and falls in love with his twin sister Dziewanna. They court, echoing many Slavic courtship rituals, culminating in their marriage at the summer solstice. This marriage would also bring a temporary truce between Perun and Veles. In this spring-summer love and marriage story, she symbolizes the life aspect of Jaryło's life-death-rebirth cycle.

OTHER NAMES:
Devana, Dziewonia

MARZANNA

MARZANNA

Marzanna is sometimes thought of merely as a Goddess of death, but she is more accurately a Goddess of death and rebirth, including the death and rebirth of nature, and she is also associated with dreams. It is said that Jaryło was unfaithful to Dziewanna in the Autumn, so she kills him for his infidelity, In doing so, she ceases to be Dziewanna the maiden and becomes Marzanna the crone or hag. After killing Jaryło, Marzanna builds herself a home out of Jaryło's body, symbolizing the start of winter. When winter ends and the spring returns, Slavic people in various countries will drown Marzanna in effigy during a festival in which they celebrate the return of Jaryło from the underworld and the rebirth of Marzanna as Dziewanna, and thus the cycle begins anew.

OTHER NAMES:

Marena, Morana, Morena, Kyselica, Maslenitsa, Mara

SELECTED BIBLIOGRAPHY:

Below is a recommended further reading and list
of reference books the author found instrumental
in doing reseach for this book. This is not the only
reference used for each subject, but the most useful
ones you may enjoy in doing further reading..

Linkner, Tadeusz. 1998.
"Słowiańskie Bogi i Demony"
A scholarly exploration of the Slavic pantheon.

Podgórscy, Barbara and Adam. 2018.
" Wielka Księga Demonów Polskich".
An encyclopedia of Polish demons,
deities, and folklore creatures.

Vargas, Witold, and Zych, Pawel. 2018.
"Bestiariusz Słowiański: Część Pierwsza i Druga"
A beautifully illustrated book
of Slavic folklore beasts.

Winiarski, Damian; Kamoń, Jan.
Słowiański Bestiariusz. 2016-2020.
https://blog.slowianskibestiariusz.pl/bestiariusz/
Articles explaining various Slavic
mythological beings (English available).

Disclaimer:

This book is a work of art. It is not intended as a scientific
manual or research source. Care was taken to ensure
information is as complete and accurate as possible, but
is in no way exhaustive or definitive.

Alex Kujawa is a graphic artist and illustrator based in the Chicago area, where she lives with her husband and cats. She was born in Poland and moved to the United States in her teens, where she attended Harper College and Judson University. Her personal style has evolved as a blending of creepy and beautiful, being inspired by the art nouveau movement, as well as horror and dark fantasy. She usually works in ink with pen and marker, and occasionally adds digital color. She has worked on a wide variety of art projects, including illustrations for "WITCH: Fated Souls" tabletop RPG by Angry Hamster Publishing, and the "Ice Zombies" comic book by Waterfoot Comics. She began her series of illustrated folklore books in 2017, but has been illustrating folklore creatures for far longer. To see more of Alex's art, follow her on social media through AlexKujawa.com

WHEEJAWA PUBLISHING
third edition, 1st printing

www.AlexKujawa.com

OTHER BOOKS IN THIS SERIES:

♥ **31 FEMALE GHOSTS, MONSTERS, & DEMONS FROM AROUND THE WORLD:**
Dives into the theme of female creatures in folktales and mythologies from around the world - ghosts, demons, monsters, and the like. This book contains 31 illustrations and background information on each particular creature.
ISBN 979-8-9866079-1-7

☠ **31 GHOST STORIES:**
Ranging from famous to more obscure and even including a personal story, this book contains 31 illustrations and background information on each particular ghost. All ghost stories are tied to places and a majority of the ghosts are named, and circumstances of their deaths explained.
ISBN 979-8-9866079-2-4

🐈 **31 SUPERNATURAL FELINES:**
The fourth in the illustrated folklore series, this book dives in to various world mythologies and folklore, introducing 31 of the most fascinating feline creatures of supernatural origin, as chosen by the artist, who tends to favor Slavic mythology.
ISBN 979-8-9866079-4-8

* 9 7 9 8 9 8 6 6 0 7 9 3 1 *